Design Science Research Methodology:
Guide for Graduate Students

By Dr. Betina Tagle

Why a DSR Methodology guide?

Design Science Research (DSR) methodology is used to create and evaluate solutions for identified information technology (IT) problems in the IT domain and organizations (19). The world is connected at a millisecond pace and technology changes daily. The world needs design to build for the future to be fast enough to keep pace! DSR is about innovation and design. It is an exciting research methodology that brings in elements of both applied and academic research, and allows for science fiction curiosities. DSR uses research beyond just engineering since some of the problems may not be solvable, or it has phenomenological aspects yet creates invaluable research for the existing knowledge-base (8, 21). DSR pushes the boundaries of computing to the edge and beyond! This is a guide to assist graduate students in where to start with using the DSR methodology. It is a beginning, a platform of information and resources to build the future!

Dr. Betina Tagle

46 University Dr

Augusta, ME 04330

betina.tagle@maine.edu

Acknowledgements

Thank you to the DSR seminal experts for your review of this guide. Your input was invaluable! The goal was to provide quality information to graduate students that are using the DSR methodology, would like to, or it can become their option. So, I appreciate the personal time you gave to the review of this guide. I had the privilege of meeting all of you at the DESRIST 2015 in Ireland and I am grateful for that experience.

Thank you!

Contents

Definition of DSR

Design means "to invent and bring into being" (17, para. 1). Thus, design deals with the creation of something new that does not exist, such as an Information Technology (IT) artifact. An artifact is "an object made by a human being" for use (16, para. 1). Therefore, DSR is about designing an object that is new to the technology industry. The intent of DSR is obtaining new knowledge while designing, creating, and researching the IT artifact.

March and Smith (1995) provided the foundation of the categories of an IT artifact, constructs, models, methods, and instantiations. The following is a list of examples of the types of artifacts that can be associated with the categories:

- An artifact can create or be an improvement: Gregor and Hevner (2013) expressed that improvement (new approach to an old problem), exaptation (old approach to a new problem), or invention (new approach to a new problem).
- An artifact can be a whole or partial solution.
- An artifact can be a routine, where the knowledge to create it exists already, or innovative, where knowledge is learned during the research: This is the deductive, inductive, and adductive aspects of a research (8).
- The artifact that is a construct is a "conceptual vocabulary of a domain";
- The artifact that is a Models is a "set of propositions or statements expressing relationship between constructs";
- The artifact that is a method is a "set of steps used to perform a task, or how-to knowledge";
- The artifact that is an instantiation is an "operationalization of a construct, a model, or a method";
- The artifact that is a theory-type is a construct that is "analogous to experimental natural sciences, coupled with reflections and abstractions" (24, pp. 13-14).

There is a distinct different between natural and design science. Simon (1996), explains that the *science of the artificial*, or man-made instantiations and phenomena, is performed to meet a required need. The design is routine if the knowledge required for meeting that need already exists. The design is only engineering if the solution to meet that need does not need research or new knowledge. Creation of an IT artifact requires new knowledge from research and innovative design. "Innovative design may call for the conduct of research to fill the knowledge gaps" (24, p. 33). Using DSR to create an IT artifact allows one to add to the knowledge base of the whole research process not just apply the knowledge base to create an artifact (11). This includes the following research:

- during the creation of the conceptual map of the topic
- the subject areas involved in the literature review
- creation of the problem statement
- creation of the research question
- the artifact creation process that is chosen
- the issues that arise while creating the artifact

By its activity then, DSR *changes the state-of-the-world* with new knowledge and innovative artifacts (24).

Purpose of DSR

The purpose of DSR is to add new knowledge to the existing technology knowledge-base. The idea is that the results of the iterative and cycled approaches of DSR are useful to practitioners (6). The goal is to provide practical relevance. If a problem can be solved with engineering alone than it is not DSR. This is important since the activity of research is to contribute to the understanding of a phenomenon and add the existing body of knowledge (1; 22).

History of DSR

This section provides a brief history of how IT research grew into the powerful research domain it is today. This manual refers to the scope used by DSR as Technology to capture all the areas that are now a part of the technological field science. The original range was information and communications technology (ICT) in corporations, which started around the 1990s. Between the 1950s and 1960s computers grew so rapidly in businesses that the research field of Management Information Systems (MIS) emerged to study its design, impact, and effects (14).

6

The need for technical expertise to manage the growth of MIS skyrocketed and by the 1980s universities and colleges had IT programs. During this time the creation of a structured IT research framework started in order to meet the academic expectations and criteria of research performance.

For research to be legitimate, it requires rigor and validity that can be measured, which means a type of methodology process must be used. The first edition of the book, *The Sciences of the Artificial*, by Simon in 1969, was the catalyst that legitimized design science. His book provided the distinction between natural and design science that justified design as a separate entity of research. Simon's idea had created the ability for designing an IT artifact as a structured research model to come to fruition; however, it was a slow growth. The turning point was the work, *Systems development in information systems research,* by Nunamaker in 1991. This work provided a definition, theory, and model for design science in research, and established the Engineering Approach method. This spurred different suggested methods, such as information systems design theory (ISDT) by Walls and authors in 1992. By the end of the 1990s, the research methodology was now considered Information System Design Research (ISDR) and a legitimate field of research.

In 2004, Hevner and DSR associates published his work on the seven principles for ISDR, which was the foundational work that established a roadmap to validate this type of research. With this validation in effect there became a need to guide the IS research community to a bigger audience. In 2006 the Design Science Research in Systems and Technology (DESRIST) annual conference was established as this vehicle. After this, two publications provided the platform to use the term Design Science Research (DSR). In 2007, Kuechler and Vaishnav's book, *Design science research methods and patterns: innovating information and communication technology,* used the descriptor Design Science Research. In 2008, Peffers', Tuunanen's, Rothenberger's, and Chatterjee's work, *A design science research methodology for information systems research,* used the descriptor Design Science Research Methodology (DSRM). The term Design Science Research is the commonly used term now within the IT research community and the academics.

Research Element

There are so many different elements that go into DSR. Research is typically conducted when knowledge is needed. Applied research is to find a solution to a problem or create something, such as a product, while basic research, sometimes known as academic, is to find out something. This can really mean that DSR straddles both of these ideas, creation and curiosity. This supports the fact that DSR does not have a conventional research question set up since it is an iterative and cycled approach. It can be a question or a problem statement, and it can change during the research because new knowledge is gained until the end. It may seem that this leaves DSR almost too flexible but this is why it is a wonderful research for designing and innovation.

Research paradigm

How to conduct the research then begins with the research paradigm that best fits in the field of study and the outcome desired. A paradigm is the understanding of how a problem is studied answered (15). According to Anderson (2013), a paradigm is based on a combination of its ontology, epistemology, and methodology. Ontology is the way reality is constructed, or "how things really are and how things really work" (4, p. 201). Epistemology is the knowledge of that reality (2). Methodology is what procedure or blueprint will be used to unearth that reality. Method is the tools used to process the methodology.

For DSR the reality of the epistemological-side of research would be to know if an IT artifact solution did answer to its associated problem. Anderson (2013) suggested the pragmatic paradigm for design-based research is focused on practice, which aligns with DSR. Hevner (2007), suggested that DSR is associated with the pragmatic nature of design science and uses the pragmatic philosophy. Pragmatism is not based on finding truth or reality, but on problem-solving, thus practice. Thus, Anderson (2013), suggested the following for the pragmatic research paradigm:

- Ontology: Reality is the practical effects of ideas;
- Epistemology: Any way of thinking/doing that leads to pragmatic solutions is useful;
- Methodology: Mixed-methods, design-based research, action research.

DSR falls within the practical frameworks of research. It is unique within research philosophies in that its research paradigm perspective changes as knowledge is gained. As research is processed through its iterative cycles, even the problem statement can change (24). The following are explanations that specifically affect the research paradigm within DSR:

- Ontology reality is that "a single, stable underlying physical reality...constrains the multiplicity of world-states";
- Epistemology knowledge "is factual and the meaning known through the construction of an artifact";
- The methodology is Design Science Research (DSR) that processes through iterations (24, p. 17).

The discussion on pragmatic paradigm is taken a step further and includes the discussion of axiology, the study of values of the research. For DSR, the research values creation instead of understanding of truth where there must be "a far higher tolerance for ambiguity than is generally acceptable in the positivist research stance" (24, p. 18). This supports that design-based research is an iterative, process focused, interventionist, multi-level, utility-oriented, and theory generative research (2). Further, this type of paradigm promotes the iterative and exploratory and evolutionary prototyping aspects of DSR, where the research continues as the artifact is implemented or used in further research. Again, the goal of DSR is to find a solution to problem within the technology field that may not be solvable, therefore, a practical research paradigm is warranted (11).

Scientific philosophies

Scientific research and its philosophies, ontology, epistemology, and methodology, is the foundation that the research community rely on in accepting a research framework as legitimate. These philosophies are well-established in the social sciences after decades of use. However, DSR is relatively new and mapping these philosophies to the more ambiguous nature of using scientific design, design science, and the science of design within a structured field of IT may cause some issues (13). DSR has a phenomenological theme, where the creation of an IT artifact does use investigative forms, such as empirical regularities and validated theories of practical science. The relationships between ontology, epistemology, and methodology for DSR can be traced when using Iivari's twelve thesis, as follows:

1. Information Systems is ultimately an applied or practical discipline (Discipline).

2. Prescriptive research is an essential part of IS as an applied or practical discipline (Discipline).

3. The design science activity of building IT artifacts is an important part of prescriptive research in IS (Discipline).

4. The primary interest of IS lies in IT applications, and therefore IS as a design science should be based on a sound ontology of IT artifacts and especially of IT applications (Ontology).

5. IS as a design science builds IT meta-artifacts that support the development of concrete IT applications (Ontology).

6. Prescriptive knowledge of IT artifacts forms a knowledge area of its own and cannot be reduced to the descriptive knowledge of theories and empirical regularities (Epistemology).

7. The resulting IT meta-artifacts essentially entail design product and design process knowledge (Epistemology).

8. The term "design theory" should be used only when it is based on a sound kernel theory (Epistemology).

9. Constructive research methods should make the process of building IT meta-artifacts disciplined, rigorous and transparent (Methodology).

10. Explication of the practical problems to be solved, the existing artifacts to be improved, the analogies and metaphors to be used, and/or the kernel theories to be applied is significant in making the building process disciplined, rigorous and transparent (Methodology).

11. IS as a design science cannot be value-free, but it may reflect means-end, interpretive or critical orientation (Ethics).

12. The values of design science research should be made as explicit as possible (Ethics) (p. 2).

Although the IT artifacts may be the interpretation of the researcher, the validity, reliability, and its value in creating them should support the scientific philosophies in a fashion that allows acceptance in the scientific community. DSR is a real and legitimate methodology, therefore, an effective means of scientific research.

Methodology

A research methodology is "a system of methods used" to perform research within a field of study (18). It describes the different activities that will be performed, such as the data collection and its analysis (12). Examples of the more commonly known research methodologies, as follows:

- Quantitative
- Qualitative
- Mixed-method
- Design Science Research
- Action Research

Methodology is chosen for the type of research that is needed for the problem or study (12). DSR is a methodology specifically for IT research.

Research Strategy

The research strategy, or blueprint, is how the research is conducted. It helps the research answer the research questions in a methodical way. The strategy is different than the methodology in that it "deals with a logical problem and not a logistical problem" (26). Examples of some of the available designs, as follows:

- Case study
- Grounded Theory
- Ethnographic study
- Non-experimental
- Longitudinal design
- Experimental

- Cross-sectional design
- Experimental (Scientific-method based)

Design is chosen based on the goal of the research. DSR has an experimental design in that it uses iterative cycles to validate a solution to a problem.

Framework

The Framework, or process model, is the structure for the logistical sequence of activities while conducting the research (19). It is the process flow of the research. There are several models created for DSR by the experts in this field of research. The most commonly known DSR models, as follows:

- **General Design Theory (GDT).**
  Takeda, H., Veerkamp, P., Tomiyama, T., and Yoshikawa, H. 1990.Modeling Design Processes. AI Magazine 11, 4, 37-48.

- **System Development Research Process.**
  Nunamaker, J.F., Jr., Chen, M., and Purdin, T.D.M. 1991.Systems Development in Information Systems Research. Journal of Management Information Systems 7, 3, 89-106.

- **Research Framework in Information Systems.** Provides the distinction of outputs and activities in research (March & Smith, 1995).
  March, S.T. and Smith, G.F. (1995). Design and natural science research on information technology. Decision Support Systems 15, 251- 266.

- **General Design Cycle (GDC).**
  Kuechler, W., Vaishnavi, V. K., & Peffer, S. (2005). The aggregate general design cycle as a perspective on the evolution of computing communities of interest. *Computing Letters*, *1*(3), 123-128.

- **Design Science Research Methodology (DSRM) process model.**
  Pfeffers, K., Tuunanen, T., Rothenberger, M. A., & Chatterjee, S. (2007). A design science research methodology for information systems research. Journal of management information systems, 24(3), 45-77.

- **Process Model for Procedurally Transparent (PMPT).**
  Gleasure, R., Feller, J., & O'Flaherty, B. F. (2012). Procedurally Transparent Design Science Research: A Design Process Model.

- **Action Design Research (ADR) process model**
  Sein, M., Henfridsson, O., Purao, S., Rossi, M., & Lindgren, R. (2011). Action design research.

Again, there are other models available and the best approach is to search online in the DSR experts and community.

Research Activities

The research activities are based on the goal of the research problem being addressed. The goal of the research may be to design an innovative idea, build an IT artifact, create a stepped process, perform validation on established science and design, repeat research from a scientific publication, create a product prototype, finding results from experimentation, or to create some research support around a phenomenological outcome, design for the future, or basic research. This is why it is important to choose a strategy and framework for the research. It is the scaffolding that structures the accepted support for the research. This does not detract from the fact that research results may be phenomenological or based on futuristic ideas that do not exist yet. However, research that will be communicated to chosen audience is still research that needs to be valid and reliable and that means diligent research. Performing research of any kind means certain things will be done throughout to create reliable and valid research, no matter how small.

The following is a list of common knowledge research activities that are used for any type of research.

- Define the problem
- Review the literature
- Formulate the problem statement or question
- Choose the research design
- Conduct the research
- Interpret the results
- Communicate the research findings

Documentation is of the utmost importance as this is the tool to perform the final step of communicating your research to its chosen audience. Find a method that is best to capture the research and consistently use it throughout. Hand-written papers, like a spiral notebook. Computer document formats, like word, spreadsheet, text-type document. Voice or video recordings. From beginning when the research question, or statement, is established, to the outcomes of the research, the research needs to be captured.

Kernel Theory in DSR

Kernel Theory is a part of DSR because the existing knowledge-base of the IT domain does lend to the inclusion of all knowledge that may directly and indirectly impact the research. It is commonly known that kernel theory is the class of theory for the natural or social sciences. There is a thought that the information system discipline (maybe now more so known as information technology) should create a design theories class, suggested by Walls, et al. (1992), *Building Information System Design Theory for Vigilant EIS.* In this paper the authors present the information system design theory (DT), where it is "to be a prescriptive theory which integrates normative and descriptive theories into design paths intended to produce more effective information systems" (p.37). The official description is that DT includes two important features, the need to build a product and the process to do such. Below is the foundation of the DT as described on page four in the Walls, et al., paper.

Design Product

1. Meta-requirements > Describes the class of goals to which the theory applies.

2. Meta-design > Describes a class of artifacts hypothesized to meet the meta-requirements.

3. Kernel theories > Theories from natural or social sciences governing design requirements

4. Testable design product hypotheses > Used test whether the meta-design satisfies the meta-requirements.

Design Process

1. Design Method > A description of procedure(s) for artifact construction.

2. Kernel theories > Theories from natural or social sciences governing design process itself.

3. Testable design process hypotheses > Used to verify whether the design method results in an artifact which is consistent with the meta-design. (p. 4).

The Design Theory is essentially the means to express the new knowledge from a DSR project for general knowledge accessibility (Kuechler, W. (2015). Dr. Keuchlers feedback email). Section *5. A Design Theory of Vigilant Information Systems* of the paper gives an example of DT for a DSR project. Let me clarify to say that this is in regards to use of DT, not how to conduct DSR itself.

The trend to fully accept DT and even create a 'design theories' class is still ongoing. Venable (2006) suggested that "higher quality research fully develops generalised knowledge in the form of theories" (p. 10). Gregor (2006) suggests that a theory is a cumulative structure of support for knowledge to substantiate research for IS/IT that seems to create artifacts that many times are trending fashionable conventions recreated. March and Smith (1995) suggested that Design Science is the goal of DSR because creating an artifact to solve problem is the goal and does not need to test theory. Hevner (2004) suggested that evaluation of an artifact is rigor and may include theory-based inclusion during the research.

As you conduct your DSR research, do not concentrate on if you are including theory, but do a thorough literature review to ensure that all aspects of subjects that touch your topic, directly and indirectly, are included.

Principles of DSR

Seven Guidelines of Dr. Hevner

The seven guidelines for DSR were created by Drs. Hevner, March, Park, and Ram, as a medium to ensure the research aligns with the intent of DSR relevance (11). These principles are provide structure to a flexible research methodology for designing innovation.

Design as an Artifact

Designing an artifact with DSR requires the production of a viable solution or improvement, or the knowledge outputs from trying to produce them (11). It needs to be purposeful and have value. It needs to answer to what business need its creation is meeting. The definition of the artifact to be created needs to support its utility. This means that it should fit within one of the categories of being a construct, model, method, or instantiation (11). DSR requires an artifact to be created and evaluated, therefore, the artifact must support its intentions of design and purpose.

Problem Relevance

DSR has the purpose of finding solutions to problems within the technology domain. The research needs to be relevant to the problem space and phenomena of this environment (11). This is to gain the appropriate and applicable knowledge needed to find solutions for technology problems. Göbel and Cronholm (2012), suggested that two knowledge requirements must be met when using DSR; 1) practical, and, 2) the new information can be used within the original knowledge-base. Therefore, the problem must be real-world in nature to meet the purpose of practical utility and add to existing knowledge. Again, the problem needs to have relevance. However, the reason for research is to examine what is known and not known about a problem and solution set in order to find the answers. To that end, DSR is that research that is particularly focused on problems that may not be solvable and cannot be answered with engineering alone (10). This sometimes can obscure the relevance of a problem and create vague DSR topics of research. A problem needs to be clearly defined in order to support its relevance.

Next is an example of what justification process may occur to validate a problem's relevance, as well as the use of DSR. A software application that records people's vital statistics the provided doctors with data that can be used to make healthcare decisions was proposed. The real-world problem defined was that doctors cannot make good diagnosis or prognosis decisions because a patient's vital statistics history is not readily available or cannot be used to do a trend analysis adequately. The software application proposed records vital statistic data for periods of time and can produce trend analysis for doctors' use. This may be a viable solution for the defined real-world problem. However, the problem can be solved by just the creation of the software application, which means that only engineering is needed. The problem may be relevant to the real-world, but it is not applicable to the use of DSR.

What would make this problem a DSR topic? The problem is linear in nature and needs an altering dynamic that requires research and examination. For example, the healthcare industry's modernization trend is that patient's medical records are created, stored, and available online to a wide variety of healthcare providers and services. This adds an altering dynamic to the problem. Although the problem may still concentrate on the fact that doctors need vital statistics data for trend analysis, the inclusion of health records being online for availability adds the question, where else does the data need to go or can the software application be used?

The problem can then be expanded to include the altering dynamic that would require the research cycles of DSR. The chosen dynamic may be that the software application needs to have the ability to upload the vital statics data into patient records that reside in different technology environments. Therefore, an application interface (API) is needed that can be used with any type of technology environment. This may be a problem that is not solvable because technology has such a vast range of factors that may involve, such as programming languages, operating systems (OS), data communication protocols, and kernel behaviors to name just a few. The goal then is to find create an API, which means choosing the programming language infrastructure that would communicate with any OS and its kernel processing. This expanded problem then would be relevant to a real-world problem, the use of DSR, and better map the relevance of artifact to problem.

Design Evaluation

In order for DSR to produce viable solutions in technology, rigorous methods of evaluation is required (10). The critical aspect of DSR is the evaluation of the artifact's ability to be the solution to the problem it was meant to solve, the research was conducted with rigor, and that the solution and problem were relevant. A failure in the evaluation does not mean that the research is a failure because DSR is to produce new knowledge that can be added to the existing knowledge base within the technology domain. DSR research is about ambiguous, phenomenological, or problems that may not seem solvable, which means that there is a good chance the evaluation will fail. This is why the evaluation is not just about the IT artifact working properly, but the applicability of new knowledge to the knowledge-base.

The technology domain may not always provide the ability to use data from a live experience because of the nature of the test criteria needed. This means that the data within the collection process cycle of research, which for DSR is the data used to perform the artifact evaluation, may be simulated data and test simulations. This type of data is used when having the appropriate test data is a significant barrier to the evaluation (5). Using the same software application artifact example, it may not be feasible to use real patient data to test the artifact because the data is protected data under the Health Insurance Portability and Accountability Act (HIPAA) of 1996. When simulation in data and testing is needed during the artifact evaluation it must be adequately justified and the process well-documented to ensure that rigor was maintained during the evaluation. Again, this is not to prove it is not valid testing, but to show it is more than valid, it is better quality testing.

Research Contributions

A contribution is needed to enhance the knowledge of the subject and research methodology when DSR is performed (10). Whether the outcome result is a success or failure the knowledge from the research is a contribution, even it supports what does not work. An example is that of Thomas Edison who failed repeatedly during his research to improve the light bulb. He did not invent the light bulb, but had a solution to improve on the light bulb, which had the problem of the short-life filament. This problem made light bulbs expensive and a luxury that not everyone could afford. After many failures, some say 1,000, he patented the "...carbon filament or strip coiled and connected to platina contact wires" that was able to bring electricity to everyone (3, pp. 2-3).

Research Rigor

DSR requires rigor to provide a working solution, not only in its evaluation, but in the construction of the artifact (10). The practical and scientific audiences need to accept the research, therefore creating a repeatability in the research is key. If DSR is to produce solutions and knowledge that can be used in the real-world, than it must have an element of repeatability. This can be from the use of industry standards during the development of the artifact, or data collection methods that have already been peer-reviewed and in use, such as a well-established user acceptance test. This is not only gives a way to repeat the research, but measurability to the rigor of the research conducted.

DSR is about researching the entirety of the ability to provide a solution to a problem and this means that the process used to create the artifact. In the course of the research it may be determined that existing models of artifact development or data collections do not work. It is possible to use models and techniques that were created during the research, however, in order to provide measureable rigor to their use they would need to go through a process of peer-review. There are some possibilities.

A researcher that developed a technique or model during the research could publish a paper on it in a peer-reviewed journal. If the research will be, or need to be completed, prior to the paper's publication it is possible to use the submitted publication as a working paper to support the use of the new technique or model. However, it is a good idea to clearly define the justification of its use in the research. Regarding the need for a better collection data method. If there is a need to adapt a version of an established method of data collection to fit the research need, than the modified version would need to go through a peer-review process prior to its use. This can be done in a field-work exercise where the method is tested on population and edited based on peer-review feedback. It is important to note that the population used in the field-work exercise cannot be used during the evaluation of the artifact.

Another point regarding population use in DSR is the possibility that it does not include human participation. DSR is research conduct in the technology domain and therefore may be system-based only. Because research typically includes human participants so generalization statement is provided to support the results, it must be noted that a system-based population may not have the ability to be generalized. However, if human participants are the population than the generalization statement must only include the population demographics used during the research. Using the software application example from above, if the research included a user acceptance test with the population demographic requirements of only nurses who have worked in an emergency room for at least 10 years, then the generalization made could only include that same population requirement.

Design as a Search Process

DSR requires a *search process* technique, or research framework (10). An example of a search process would be the *experiments and exploration* framework, which is one of the search patterns suggestion in the book, *Design science research methods and patterns: innovating information and communication technology* by Vaishnavi and Kuechler, 2007. The experiments and exploration framework is the search process that will use repeated cycles of experiments to explore the best way to create the artifact. However, it also must follow the rules and laws of the domain where the problem space and knowledge base exist. Using the software application example from above, this could be the healthcare or medical technology domain.

Communication of Research

The results and outputs of DSR research need to be communicated in a usable fashion (10). The typical process for research communication is through journal publications and conference presentations. The key is that research and its material are peer-reviewed, which provides a form of validity. With the need for researchers to publish their research so it can be used and the modern trend of online availability, open access journals as acceptable communication vehicles is acceptable. However, these must be used with caution in order to ensure that the open access journal does have a peer-review process and provides quality research publications. According to Dr. Venable's communication to me during the DESRIST 2015 conference, in Dublin Ireland, IEEE is an example of an appropriate open access journal.

The software application artifact example used for the seven guidelines of DSR shows how the principles within a DSR principle set builds upon one another. Answering each principle within the DSR principle set chosen by the researcher will produce either support for or against the topic being a good fit for DSR. This is a critical step for research problems and solutions in the technology domain because of its nature towards practical knowledge of a phenomenological nature, which can be contradictive. Is may seem that an artifact that requires utility cannot be created with the spirit of innovation. However, DSR encompasses not just producing an artifact, but the new knowledge in its production. The idea in answering to each to the principles within a DSR principle set is not to discourage DSR research, but rather to fully define the problem and solution so it can support the validity, reliability, and acceptance required within the scientific community. It is a mechanism for quality control in DSR research.

Three-cycle principles of Dr. Hevner

Another established DSR principle set is the three-cycle principles that include the Relevance cycle, Design cycle, and Rigor cycle. These provide "clear and consistent definitions, ontologies, boundaries, guidelines, and deliverables for the design and execution of high quality design science research projects" (10, p. 87). Principles are away to ensure the ambiguity that may exist in DSR research is supported by research. The principles used need to fit the scope of the research and the skills of the researcher. Therefore, it may be that this set of principles offer its use towards DSR research conducted for creating an artifact for an improvement solution, or a researcher that has the skill-level to interpret the level of rigor needed in research without a detailed instructional roadmap. A graduate student researcher may need the more in-depth principles the seven Guidelines offer. However, the goal of principles is to support rigor in research and this is a good option to meet this goal.

Relevance Cycle

This cycle is to apply the context of the research for design science as inputs and outputs and verify that the evaluation is appropriate (10). This cycle is to ensure that research remains within its domain no matter the iterations of testing, development, and feedback that is acquired. However, when it comes to the need for further research, the use of other methodologies are encouraged to support the relevance of the research (10). These other methodologies can provide any deficiencies that may need to be supported by quantitative or qualitative studies. This cycle provides the boundaries for the research goal.

Design Cycle

This cycle is the key to research in design science and initiates the loop between the construction, evaluation, and feedback to further refine the artifact (10). The nature of this cycle is to generate and evaluate requirements and alternate requirements until a design is known that satisfies those requirements (24). This iteration of the research is where the actually work to create the artifact is done. Relevance testing can take place here to ensure that the research stay within its intended goal. Rigor plays a part in the development of the IT artifact, where laboratory tests are used to document that the research is grounded on solid arguments appropriately (10). This cycle can have multiple iterations in order to ensure that the design of the artifacts meet relevance and rigor criteria.

Rigor Cycle

Rigor is especially paramount within DSR to show that a solution is not just using engineering, or is not routine. Knowledge is the key to this cycle. Past knowledge must be known and use a proper depth of the existing knowledge-base of theories and engineering (10). To add to the body of knowledge, DSR must show that research was performed at a great depth. This is found in the existing meta-level information about the artifact (10).

A question that often arises in DSR is if theory is necessary to prove rigor. No, because this can hinder the idea that design science is meant to research phenomena in technology, provide innovative solutions, and solve problems. Although, being able to use theory to create research ideas is a worthy process (10). The key to rigor is that the research needs to be grounded in solid problems and arguments for acceptance; however, for DSR to meet its broad expanse of research scope creativity is warranted. According to Hevner (2007), DSR knowledge ".... will include any extensions to the original theories and methods made during the research, the new meta-artifacts (design products and processes), and all experiences gained from performing the research and field testing the artifact in the application environment" (p. 90).

Because principles of DSR is to provide a roadmap to ensure rigor and appropriate research scope of a problem, the principles used need to have an appropriate depth. It is noticed that the three-cycle principle set has the support of rigor up front, whereas the Seven Guideline principle set methodically builds on its rigor. The goal of DSR is to provide innovative solutions to problems that are phenomenological nature, therefore, use of any of these principle sets is warranted.

One-cycle principle of Drs. Winter and Albani

This one-cycle principle may offer the ability for DSR to be used specifically within an organization, or an artifact being created for an improvement. The idea behind this principle set is that organizations have "purposefully designed and implemented systems" that are specific to meet a business process (26, p. 64). This one-cycle iteration provides the use of DSR to perform a change or improvement when only re-design is needed. This principle also grew out of the idea that Hevner's three-cycle view overlaps the rigor in each cycle, but separate cycles do not have to be created for this to occur (26).

The one cycle contains the required DSR activities of design and evaluation. During this process there are two DSR knowledge base search processes occurring between the activities, application scope, and artifact character (26). The goal is that each iteration of the one-cycle provides the ability to revisit the knowledge-base of the problem space in its domain. This is the foundation of DSR, that the research creates new knowledge not only from the artifact, but from creating the artifact.

DSR is research of the technology domain and it its growth pattern provides an abundant supply of problems that needs practical solutions. DSR is design and science and science must follow the laws of its domain. Principles of DSR can provide a measurability for this requirement. They also provide the support of acceptance of DSR within the science community.

Artifact of DSR

The IT artifact by DSR can be different solutions created to solve, or improve, a problem. Again, artifacts call within one of the following categories:

- Constructs: are syntax and semantic for a domain, such as classification system, language standards, or ontologies;
- Models: relations between construct elements, such as meta models, or reference models;
- Method: algorithms and proceedings within a problem area, such as, approaches for business process modeling or software development;
- Instantiation: concrete representation of a construct, model, or method to use in testing a concept for real-world knowledge;
- Theory: description of cause and effect (24, pp. 13-14).

Prototype

An artifact can be a prototype in any category and can have different definitions based on the use in the research; however, the main use in technology has been for software development. Pressman (1997), provides some examples of types of prototypes, as follows:

- Throwaway, or Rapid Prototyping: is used to understand the requirements needed for a problem;

- Evolutionary: is used to build a functioning artifact so it can be used after the research;

- Incremental: small prototypes are built for different functions and then combined as a whole artifact.

This is not a full list of available prototype definitions, but it at least provides an awareness of what prototypes can be considered for an artifact within DSR.

Artifact Evaluation

The evaluation of the artifact is a key activity within DSR since the creation of an artifact as its research methodology. The evaluation of an artifact is to test if it answers the research question. Keep in mind that DSR supports researching problems that may not be solvable and to that end the answer to the research question may be no. However, in situations like this the new knowledge is the key. If it adds to the body of knowledge than the research was of value. As in the example of Thomas Edison, although he was able to find the answer to his research question, he also failed many times. The artifact could be seen as the suggested improved filament of a light build because he was looking to extend the life of the light build. He has a specific research question and artifacts that had to be tested. If he had stopped after the 600 test cycle would have his research been a failure? No, because it showed what not work to his specific research questioned so it was valuable new knowledge. This does not mean that all research questions that have a no answer is good research. What this means is that if the research is conducted with rigor and validity and the new knowledge is of value to the existing knowledge than it is valuable research.

Communication of a DSR Paper

The presentation of an IT artifact and its research is important to the IT and science community so communicating it is critical. Gregor & Hevner (2013) provide a pathway that provides how to communicate research in their paper *Positioning and presenting design science research for maximum impact*, listed as below:

1. appreciate the levels of artifact abstractions that may be DSR contributions,
2. identify appropriate ways of consuming and producing knowledge when they are preparing journal articles or other scholarly works,
3. understand and position the knowledge contributions of their research projects, and
4. structure a DSR article so that it emphasizes significant contributions to the knowledge base (p. 337).

To continue with Gregor & Hevner (2013), they suggest that artifacts and research have different maturity levels in the artifact's solution and application, the picture below (with permission) shows the maturity level framework.

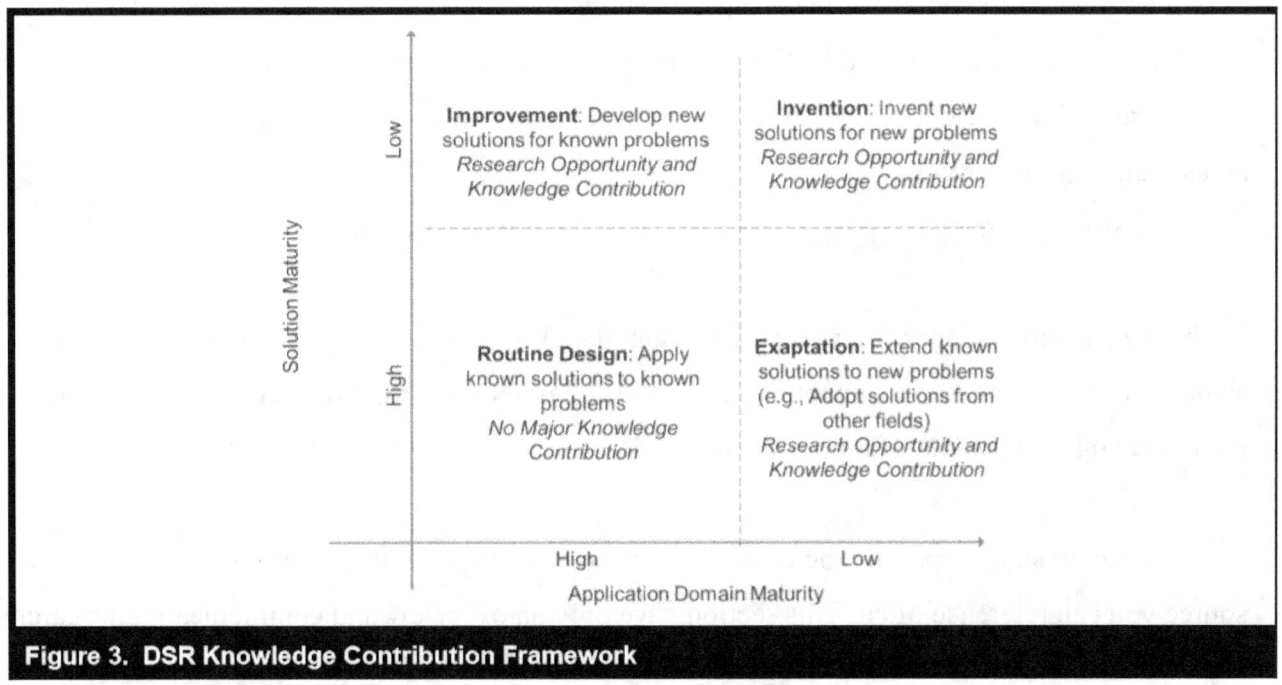

Figure 3. DSR Knowledge Contribution Framework

(Gregor & Hevner, 2013, *Positioning and presenting design science research for maximum impact*, p 345).

Categorizing an artifact and its research into the maturity framework provides the researcher a measurement of depth to the knowledge that was added or touched. This can help the researcher write a research paper that helps explain the right information to the intended audience. This is an incredible tool for presenting research.

Gregor & Hevner (2013) include an example of an outline of a DSR research paper by chapter, as follows:

1. *Introduction* - Problem definition, problem significance/motivation, introduction to key concepts, research questions/objectives, scope of study, overview of methods and findings, theoretical and practical significance, structure of remainder of paper.

2. *Literature Review* - Prior work that is relevant to the study, including theories, empirical research studies and findings/reports from practice.

3. *Method* - The research approach that was employed.

4. *Artifact Description* - A concise description of the artifact at the appropriate level of abstraction to make a new contribution to the knowledge base.

5. *Evaluation* - Evidence that the artifact is useful.

6. *Discussion* - Interpretation of the results: what the results mean and how they relate back to the objectives stated in the Introduction section. Can include: summary of what was learned, comparison with prior work, limitations, theoretical significance, practical significance, and areas requiring further work.

7. *Conclusions* - Concluding paragraphs that restate the important findings of the work.

Each chapter provides specific information about the DSR that allows a researcher to give the right amount of depth to each chapter that is needed based on the maturity level category from the knowledge contribution framework (please see picture on previous page).

I highly suggest putting the Gregor & Hevner (2013) paper into your collection as a source you can reference often. This section gave only an overview and communicating research is so critical. You can find it on Google Scholar using the below citation:

Gregor, S., & Hevner, A. R. (2013). Positioning and presenting design science research for maximum impact. MIS quarterly, 337-355.

Final Thoughts

DSR is very in-depth and this manual only provides a starting point. It is best to do some exploration in literature to get a better understanding of the details in conducting this type of research. Another good sources is looking at dissertations that used DSR as its methodology.

Sources

Excellent books and articles as a starting point to understanding DSR, as follows:

- *Design science research methods and patterns: innovating information and communication technology*, a book by Vijay Vaishnavi & Bill Kuechler, 2007.
- *Design research in information systems: theory and practice*, a book by Alan Hevner & Samir Chatterjee, 2010.
- *Design science research post Hevner et al.: criteria, standards, guidelines, and expectations*, an article by Dr. Venable.

Rigor

The key to DSR is rigor because unlike qualitative and quantitative, the process of studying existing issues, DSR is creating something. The following are points to remember when performing research within design science:

- it cannot be just engineering;
- external research must be included;
- the output, an artifact, but be relevant;
- it is encouraged to use other methodologies;
- the artifact must have value;
- the evaluation must answer to the artifact requirements.

Inclusions

Within DSR there may be added processes to include in order to complete the research. For example, to develop a software solution a Software Development Life Cycle (SDLC) may need to be used to create a software type artifact.

US and Europe

Between the US and Europe the DSR usage has slight differences. This is mentioned to provide awareness of this aspect during further research of this methodology.

DSR dissertation

Writing a DSR dissertation may require additional chapters or further formatting. A university typically will typically provide an outline of the criteria that is followed to meet all the different research methodologies.

Continuing questions

There is a continuing question within the DSR community that is interesting and is provided here to spurn curiosity and research. What does instantiation really mean? How do the different definitions affect DSR? A couple good articles for this:

- A good view into the updates that has occurred with DSR since 2004, can be found in the article by Dr. Venable,
- Gregor, S., & Hevner, A. R. (2013). Positioning and presenting design science research for maximum impact. *MIS quarterly, 37*(2).
- Myers, M. D., & Venable, J. R. (2014). A set of ethical principles for design science research in information systems. *Information & Management, 51*(6), 801-809.

Resources

This manual provides an overview of DSR and is limited to the scope of experience by one graduate student's research experience. DSR is an exciting methodology and can be used easily in academics and in industry as a practitioner's tool. The following provides some resources to start:

- General References on Design Science Research:
  Http://desrist.org/desrist/content/drCitations.htm
- Design Society: https://www.designsociety.org
- Design Research Society: http://www.designresearchsociety.org
- Converis: http://converis.thomsonreuters.com/

Suggestions

The following are some suggestions where it promotes what is learned and yourself as you move further into your program, or afterwards.

- Apply to be a reviewer at conferences for the areas that you feel you are an expert. This can be for papers, posters, presentations, and even scholarship applications. This allows a knowledge-base to see what subjects are out there, how design science research is used, how papers, posters, and presentations are written, and the audience.
- Submit your topic as a paper, or a research-in-progress paper, or a poster to a conference. This allows you to see how the process works and gives opportunities to promote your topic.
- Attend a conference in the area of your topic or one you are interested in. It does not have to be a pricey conference, it can be local.

References

1. Abecker, A., Bernardi, A., Hinkelmann, K., Kühn, O., &Sintek, M. (1997, March). Towards a well-founded technology for organizational memories. In Proceedings of the AAAI Spring Symposium on Artificial Intelligence in Knowledge Management (pp. 24-26).
2. Anderson, T. (2013). Research paradigms: Ontology's, Epistemologies & Methods. Retrieved from http://www.slideshare.net/eLearnCenter/research-methods-uoc-2013.
3. Edison, T. A. (1880). U.S. Patent No.US223898 A. New Jersey: U.S. Patent and Trademark Office.
4. Fontana, A., Frey, J. H., Denzin, N. K., & Lincoln, Y. S. (1998). Collecting and interpreting qualitative materials. Interviewing: The art of science, 47-78.
5. Glasser, J., & Lindauer, B. (2013, May). Bridging the Gap: A Pragmatic Approach to Generating Insider Threat Data. In Security and Privacy Workshops (SPW), 2013 IEEE (pp. 98-104). IEEE.
6. Göbel, H., & Cronholm, S. (2012). Design science research in action-experiences from a process perspective.
7. Gregor, S. (2006). The nature of theory in information systems. MIS quarterly, 611-642.
8. Gregor, S., & Hevner, A. R. (2013). Positioning and presenting design science research for maximum impact. MIS quarterly, 337-355.
9. Hassan, N. R. (2014). Value of IS research: Is there a crisis? Communications of the Association for Information Systems, 34(41), 801-816.
10. Hevner, A. R. (2007). A three cycle view of design science research. *Scandinavian journal of information systems*, *19*(2), 4.
11. Hevner, A. R., March, S. T., Park, J., & Ram, S. (2004). Design science in information systems research. MIS quarterly, 28(1), 75-105.
12. Howell, K. E. (2013) Introduction to the Philosophy of Methodology. London: Sage Publications.
13. Iivari, J. (2010). Twelve theses on design science research in information systems. In *Design Research in Information Systems* (pp. 43-62).Springer US.
14. Kuechler, B., & Vaishnavi, V. (2008). On theory development in design science research: anatomy of a research project. European Journal of Information Systems, 17(5), 489-504.
15. Kuhn, T. S. (1962). The Structure of Scientific Revolutions Vol.
16. Merriam-Webster. (2015a). Artifact. Retrieved from http://www.merriam-webster.com/dictionary/artifact.
17. Merriam-Webster. (2015b). Design. Retrieved from http://www.merriam-webster.com/dictionary/design.
18. Method. (2015). Method. Retrieved from https://www.google.com/#q=what+is+methodology.
19. Model. (2015). Model. Retrieved from https://www.google.com/#q=what+is+a+model+.
20. Pfeffers, K., Tuunanen, T., Rothenberger, M. A., & Chatterjee, S. (2007). A design science research methodology for information systems research. *Journal of management information systems*, *24*(3), 45-77.
21. Pressman, R. S. (1997). Software Engineering: A practical approach. McGraw-Hill.
22. Simon, H. (1996). The Sciences of the Artificial. MIT Press.

23. Tagle, B., & Felch, H. (2015). Exploring an agent as an economic insider threat solution. In *Proceedings of the 10th International Conference, DESRIST 2015. Dublin, Ireland, 20-22 May. pp. 1-8*. Springer.
24. Vaishnavi, V. K., & Kuechler Jr, W. (2007). Design science research methods and patterns: innovating information and communication technology. CRC Press.
25. Venable, J. (2006, February). The role of theory and theorising in design science research. In Proceedings of the 1st International Conference on Design Science in Information Systems and Technology (DESRIST 2006) (pp. 1-18).
26. Winter, R., & Albani, A. (2013). Restructuring the design science research knowledge base.In *Designing Organizational Systems* (pp. 63-81).Springer Berlin Heidelberg.
27. Yin, R. (1989). Case Study Research: Design and Methods (Applied Social Research Methods). SAGE Publications, Inc.

www.ingramcontent.com/pod-product-compliance
Lightning Source LLC
Chambersburg PA
CBHW081316180526
45170CB00007B/2729